WINTER JOURNEY
EL VIAJE DEL INVIERNO

Alicia Aza
Translated by J. Kates and Stephen A. Sadow

ČERVENÁ BARVA PRESS
SOMERVILLE, MASSACHUSETTS

Copyright © 2020
Spanish Text © Alicia Aza

All rights reserved. No part of this book may be reproduced in any manner without written consent except for the quotation of short passages used inside of an article, criticism, or review.

Červená Barva Press
P.O. Box 440357
W. Somerville, MA 02144-3222

www.cervenabarvapress.com
Bookstore: www.thelostbookshelf.com

Cover Art: Michèle Oliva
Cover Design: William J. Kelle
Production: Steve Asmussen

ISBN: 978-1-950063-36-9

Library of Congress Control Number: 2020931115
Distributed by Small Press Distribution: www.spdbooks.org

"Stalagmites in the Winter Garden" was previously published in *Cyphers*, #78.
Robert Walser translation by Christopher Middleton.

WINTER JOURNEY
EL VIAJE DEL INVIERNO

Table of Contents

I   **The Pathways of the Senses**
       Las Rutas de los Sentidos

Los Viajes Transparentes   4
Transparent Journeys

Cartografía del Tiempo   6
Cartography of Time

El Murmullo de los Pesares   8
The Murmur of Regrets

Palabras de Escarcha   10
Words of Frost

Estalagmitas en el Jardín De Invierno   12
Stalagmites in the Winter Garden

La Sinfonía del Agua   14
The Symphony of Water

Donde Habita Tu Recuerdo   16
Where Your Memory Resides

El Cauce de los Días   18
The Riverbed of Days

II   Echoes of Distance
Los Ecos De La Distancia

Azaroso Destino   22
Hazardous Fate

Las Huellas de Tu Sombra   24
The Traces of Your Shadow

Estampa de Invierno Exótico   26
Picture of Exotic Winter

El Brillo de la Nieve Tibia   28
The Brilliance of Lukewarm Snow

La Serena Bruma de las Horas   30
The Serene Haze of the Hours

El Mar de Nuestro Regreso   32
The Sea of Our Return

Larga Espera   34
Long Wait

Un Secreto Insomne   36
A Sleepless Secret

III Views of Winter
Las Miradas del Invierno

Los Límites Helados de Tu Ausencia — 40
The Frozen Boundaries of Your Absence

Paseo por la Nostalgia — 42
I Stroll Through Nostalgia

Los Sonidos Ensordecidos del Olvido — 44
The Deafening Sounds of Oblivion

Las Pisadas del Frío — 46
The Footsteps Of The Cold

Luz en el Invernadero — 48
Light in the Greenhouse

La Nieve de Tu Memoria — 50
The Snow of Your Memory

Sueños Premonitorios — 52
Premonitory Dreams

Winterreise — 54
Winterreise

About the Author — 57
About the Translators — 59

Ich kann zu meiner Reisen
Nicht wählen mit der Zeit,
Muß selbst den Weg mir weisen
In dieser Dunkelheit.

Wilhelm Müller

I can not choose
the timing of my journey,
I have to find my own way
Through this darkness.

Winter Journey pays homage to the Schubert lieder cycle *Winterrreise*, inspired by twenty-four poems of the German Romantic poet Wilhelm Müller. Like this lieder cycle, the theme of the book and its poetic tension revolve around death and winter landscapes, where I intend to create a speech in which my "lyrical" voice adopts a very specific existential positioning, shown from the very first poem ("Transparent Journeys"), and achieving a tranquility reached only through the beauty of nature.

The last poem presents death as the existential end of a journey. I use "the journey" to talk about life and "winter" to talk about death.

Winter Journey is intended to be a romantic book in which I use as metaphors those elements exalted by the Romantics: forests, mountains, caves, rocks, water, lakes, rivers, fences, ravens and the figure of the "walker". The figure of the Walker in Müller's *Winterreise* is an abandoned lover. A hiker in solitude, his dialogue occurs with introspection in a field in which only appear his tears, his broken heart, and the landscape. In my winter journey the narrator talks to a female figure with whom he has a relationship, one which could encompass any kind of love with somebody who is slowly dying.

As a counterpoint, the book also includes various descriptive poems which act as necessary pauses and stops along the way.

Alicia Aza

I
The Pathways of the Senses
Las Rutas de los Sentidos

Los Viajes Transparentes

Perpetuos caminantes sin regreso
por montañas y bosques deambulamos
desprovistos de luz que nos sorprenda
aristas destronadas de la lluvia.
Sólo queda la estela de compases
en altar de la juventud rota
con tus cabellos blancos sin deseos.
Encenderemos lumbre con retazos
del baldaquín de tus ojos dormidos
abrigo en el paseo sin estrellas
peñascos melodiosos de oraciones.
Quedará en la memoria de mis llantos
la música del hielo entre los dedos
versos a la deriva del mañana
sangre que pinta los paisajes verdes
fértil alumbramiento de un suspiro.
Descansaremos ante la belleza
en el viaje por las dunas que laten
en los surcos de las sombras confusas
perpetuos caminantes sin regreso.

Transparent Journeys

Perpetual wayfarers without return
we wander through mountains and forests
deprived of light that may surprise us
ridges eroded by the rain.
There remains only the backwash of chords
on the altar of broken youth
your white hair without desires.
We will light our way with scraps
from the canopy of your sleeping eyes
shelter in the starless passageway
the melodious outcroppings of prayer.
The music of ice under my feet
will remain in the memory of my tears
verses drifting away from tomorrow
blood that paints landscapes green
fertile illumination of a sigh.
We'll rest in the presence of beauty
on the journey through dunes that pulse
in the furrows of jumbled shadow
Perpetual wayfarers without return.

Cartografía del Tiempo

Somos viajeros libres de la vida
nómadas con maletas de inquietudes
por la senda que llora bajo el cielo
engalanado de promesas nobles.
En la eternidad de tus ojos grises
despiertas en la noche sin embozo
y arrastras los deseos inconclusos
brújula de una cueva de pasiones.
Recorro tu mirada empedernida
por el mapa que tú misma construyes
y busco ese lugar de arquitecturas
que sólo lleve el nombre de tu tiempo.
Somos esclavos fieles de la muerte
que llega sedentaria del remanso
y difumina las heladas horas
en los inviernos de la verdad blanca.

Cartography of Time

We are unfettered travelers through life
Nomads with our baggage of worries
along a path that weeps under a sky
garlanded with well-founded promises.
In the eternity of your gray eyes
you wake at night, throw off the covers
and drag your unconsummated desires
compass of a cavern of passions.
I survey your gaze hardened
by the map that you yourself construct
and I search for the site of architectures
that may bear only the naming of your time.
We are faithful slaves of the death
that arrives with the stillness of a bower
and blurs the outlines of icy hours
during the winters of white truth.

El Murmullo de los Pesares

> *Tus caricias son sueño,*
> *entreabren la muerte,*
> *son lunas accesibles,*
> *son la vida más alta.*
>
> Luis Cernuda

Estás en los umbrales de la ausencia
reja de pesadumbre desvalida
en la atalaya del adiós postrero
que divisa serena tu mirada.
La vida es un enjambre de pesares
murmullo que tus manos acarician
y rompen eslabones de las puertas
en el jardín de sueños olvidados.
Te imagino pretérita en el vuelo
reposada en un bosque de azaleas
cantora del deshielo victorioso
anaquel de virtudes ensalzadas.
Nos quedaremos ciegas en los cauces
de un viaje que se extingue sin visados
con el tacto de dudas que se mezclan
tinta negra marchita con las hojas.

¿Quién sustituirá tus manos fecundas?

The Murmur of Regrets

Your caresses are dream,
half-opening to death
they are accessible moons
they are the highest life.
Luis Cernada

You are on the thresholds of absence
a grillwork of worthless sorrowing
in the watchtower of a later farewell
that distinguishes the serenity of your gaze.
Life is a gathering of regrets
a murmur that your hands caress
and break apart the door-hinges
in the garden of forgotten dreams.
I imagine you earlier in flight
at rest now in a forest of azaleas
the singer of a triumphant thaw
trellis of exalted virtues.
We will remain blind in the course
of a journey that ends without visas
with the contact of doubts that mix
faded black ink with the foliage.

Who will replace your fruitful hands?

Palabras de Escarcha

Eres sol retenido en el crepúsculo
del invierno de tus días descalzos
que hicieron prisioneras tus mañanas
de ciegos despertares a la vida.
Tus ojos te mendigan amapolas
que recuerdan la infancia sin consuelo
poseedora de tu dicha distante.
Hoy sólo te mantienen los zumbidos
de los recuerdos de tus pies mojados
en agua que se vierte por escarcha
en la orilla de las palabras tenues.
Pronto llegará la noche serena
y el cielo teñirá cromado tono
de soledad velada con tu gesto.

Words of Frost

You are sun stuck in the twilight
of the winter of your barefoot days
that take your mornings prisoner
of blind awakenings to life.
Your eyes beg for poppies
that recall inconsolable childhood
possessor of your far-off good fortune.
Today only the buzzings continue
of memories of your feet soaked
by water run-off from the frost
on the riverbank of tentative words.
Soon the quiet night will arrive
and the sky will take on the chrome tint
of solitude veiled by your expression.

Estalagmitas en el Jardín de Invierno

No sentirás más frio
tras la excelsa vianda
ni palparás los huesos
de los frutos cortados
siervos de tu deleite.
Se extinguirán las rutas
de la gélida niña
con los brazos que roban
en el jardín de invierno.
Quedará una violeta
rival de tu vigilia
puñal de tus temores.
Y perderás el brillo
de las lágrimas ciegas
estalagmitas tristes
de la flor de febrero.

Stalagmites in the Winter Garden

You will no longer feel cold
after such sublime food
nor will you finger the stones
of harvested fruit
serving your pleasure.
The pathways of the chilled
girl with thieving hands
in the winter garden
will come to an end.
A violet will remain
rival of your vigil
dagger of your fears.
And you will lose the luster
of blind tears
sad stalagmites
of February's flower.

La Sinfonía del Agua

El ala de una hormiga solitaria
anuncia su llegada inoportuna
por unos campos húmedos con heno
que crecen y la llaman salvadora.

Bajo el eco de los cielos movidos
agujas penetrantes de un presagio
deviene turbulento con temores
que desbordan los cauces de otras vidas.
Decide ser pareja de La Estrella
y muestra siete piernas prolongadas
de colores al margen de las modas
imagen que hacen suya los amantes.

Pronuncia la tristeza de la muerte
frustra el día señalado de los novios
impide que los niños sueñen cuentos
que recuerdan cosechas oprimidas.
Ilumina los cielos por las noches
empuja sobre la gente y sus casas
remueve los olores bajo tierra
pervierte la quietud de los mortales.

A su paso el silencio brilla fresco
y un caracol divisa expectativa
en presencia de obreras voladoras
bañadas de fragante transparencia.

Y mis zapatos se hunden en el suelo
con los brotes del agua renovada.

The Symphony of Water

The wing of a solitary ant
announces its untimely arrival
over some fields wet with growing
hay that call it a savior.

Under the echo of unstable skies
penetrating needles of a harbinger
becomes turbulent with fears
overflowing the channels of other lives.
Decides to be a partner of The Star
and show seven elongated legs
with colors on the edge of fashion
lovers that make the image their own.

It declares the sadness of death
forestalls the day appointed for the couple
keeps the children from dreaming stories
that recall beaten down harvests.
It lights up the sky at night
presses down on people and their houses
stirs up odors from underground
perverts the tranquillity of mortals.

In its wake silence shines fresh
and a snail distinguishes expectation
in the presence of flying workers
bathed in fragrant transparency.

And my shoes sink into the ground
with outpourings of new water.

Donde Habita Tu Recuerdo

Tus labios son cilindros de silencio
que ruedan por un cuerpo escurridizo.
Tus ojos un cordón de cataratas
de agua gris estancada sin orillas.
Tu rostro alcanfor chino en papel seda
al resguardo del paso de los años.

Tus piernas son las letras diagonales
del tesoro que nadie fortifica.
Tus pies una biznaga de ilusiones
que caminan por sendas indelebles.
Tus manos unos hilos de contrastes
enredos de un ovillo de susurros.

¿Dónde moras con alma protectora?
¿En el desván cubierto de castañas
que Afrodita asará con fiel destreza?

Una hendidura se abre en mi recuerdo.

Where Your Memory Resides

Your lips are cylinders of silence
that spin along a slippery body.
Your eyes a string of cascades
of gray water dammed up without banks.
Your face Chinese camphor in silk paper
protected from the passing of years.

Your legs are slanted letters
from a treasure that nobody guards.
Your feet a cactus of illusions
That walk along indelible paths.
Your hands threads of contrasts
tangled into a ball of sighs.

Where do you dwell with your sheltering soul?
In the attic covered with chestnuts
that Aphrodite roasts with devoted skill?

A fissure opens in my memory.

El Cauce de los Días

Observo tu sonrisa
ávida de recuerdos
que la memoria errante
me nombra cautelosa
como sol en la bruma
máscara resignada.

Me reconoces sólo
por mis ojos ahogados
en la inmensidad propia
del cauce de los días
que desbordan afanes
crepúsculo de un nido.

Me preguntas quien era
entre fotos antiguas
que el tiempo ha convertido
en la única causa
de soportar la vida
que raptó tu linaje.

Y es tu piel quien me pide
volver con las mañanas
y observar tu sonrisa
para contar recuerdos
quimera de las celdas
que tus pliegues ocultan.

The Riverbed of Days

I observe your smile
eager for memories
that wandering recall
labels me cautious
like the sun in mist
relegated to a mask.

You recognize me only
by my drowned eyes
in the fitting immensity
of the flow of days
expressing aspirations
the twilight of a nest.

You ask me who it was
in the old photographs
that time has converted
into the only reason
to endure the life
that snatched away your heritage.

And it is your skin that asks me
to return with the mornings
and observe your smile
to go over the memories
chimera of cubicles
that your creases hide.

II
Echoes of Distance
Los Ecos De La Distancia

Azaroso Destino

Eres ese recodo de la rosa
genocidio de la belleza eterna
que hiere con la joven amante
las pasiones desconocidas.

Cuando el destino marca los senderos
te muestras prisionera en un espacio
recóndito, presencia inútil
que aguarda en constante inasible.

Habrás de venir luego con prudencia
a enterrar un destino que fue vida
donde las aves migratorias
dejaron de batir sus alas.

Has hecho reclinar las ilusiones.
¡Frívola predadora de costumbres!
Del azar eres tesorera.
Ven y hazla tuya para siempre.

Hazardous Fate

You are the curvature of the rose
genocide of eternal beauty
who afflict the young lover
with unknown passions.

When fate marks out paths
you appear as a prisoner in a hidden
space, a useless presence
who watches always out of reach.

Later you may come warily
to bury a fate that was life
where migratory birds
still their beating wings.

You made illusions withdraw.
Playful predator of customs!
You are the treasurer of hazard.
Come and make it yours forever.

Las Huellas de Tu Sombra

¡Lento enmudecer! ¡Brote de silencio!
Ya no escucharé tus cantos dorados,
desvelo de los días que cohabitan.

Has construido un paisaje intransitable
laberinto trenzado de decoros,
oculto caligrama en aguas blancas.

Recordaré tu vuelo en horizontes
ebrios de sol, calmante de los años
perdidos tras las huellas de tu sombra.

Tu cuerpo ya maduro se sumerge
en memoria nublada. Sólo quedan
tus ojos marchitados que sonríen.

Rítmica mariposa de alas rotas
pósate y sedimenta los pesares
fugitivos de la vida transida.

The Traces of Your Shadow

Slow to fall silent! Bud of silence!
I will no longer listen to your golden songs,
sleeplessness of days that live together.

You have built an impassable landscape
a labyrinth intertwined with good manners,
hidden concrete poetry in white waters.

I will remember your flight into horizons
drunk with sun, soothing the lost years
behind the traces of your shadow.

Your fully ripe body submerges itself
in cloudy memory. Only your
dried up eyes remain, smiling.

Alight, rhythmic butterfly with broken wings
and calm the fugitive troubles
of a life overwhelmed by suffering.

Estampa de Invierno Exótico

Los mercados de la urbe
vierten el olor rancio
de luces presuntuosas,
joyas de la mentira
en el viento de especias,
émulo de la nieve,
silbo de los reclamos
a rezos infinitos
en las mezquitas blancas.
Tu recuerdo se esconde
tras las fuentes dolientes
de cada pie desnudo,
verdugo de las penas
en el paisaje gélido
de arabescos azules.
Y te miro periplo
en el placer exótico
de los puestos de fruta
con ecos rebosantes.
Un gajo de naranja
solitario en el suelo,
redime los enigmas
de la vida que surge;
y su jugo se expande
por lugares con lluvia
que siembran tu memoria.

Picture of Exotic Winter

The city markets
give off a rancid odor
of presumptuous lights,
deceptive jewels
in a wind of spices
rivaling snow,
sibilance of calls
to infinite prayers
in the white mosques.
Your memory hides
behind the painful fountains
of each bare foot,
the executioner of troubles
in a cold countryside
of blue arabesques.
I watch you on an expedition
among the exotic pleasure
of fruit stands
with overflowing echoes.
A single segment
of orange on the ground
Redeems the enigmas
of burgeoning life;
and its juice spreads
with the rain through places
that seed remembrance of you.

El Brillo de la Nieve Tibia

Esculpo mi silencio frágil
sobre la urgencia de la noche
y la luz de la nieve tibia
que perfilas en la distancia.
Y busco verdad en tu boca
ardiente aposento del llanto
con caricias del crudo frío
que cristaliza por mis piernas.
El olvido siempre me guía
tras la muralla de los sueños
que transitan entre los ojos
de tus más profundos abismos.

The Brilliance of Lukewarm Snow

I sculpt my fragile silence
on the urgency of night
and the light of lukewarm snow
you adorn in the distance.
And I seek truth in your mouth
ardent bedchamber of tears
with caresses of raw cold
crystallizing on my legs.
Forgetfulness forever guides me
behind the wall of dreams
that move between the eyes
of your most profound depths.

La Serena Bruma de las Horas

Los cuerpos agrietados me conminan
a vislumbrar el sol del tiempo inerte
en la serena sombra de las horas
que discurren en los curvos mensajes
del acordeón rojizo con los pechos
apagados por su torso desnudo.
Bajo su piel emerge la distancia
con sueños destrozados que disipan
la locuaz persistencia de leyendas
de complicados ritos y memorias.
Sólo me reconfortan los perfiles
de restos olvidados y remotos
que sobreviven en los pensamientos
de tu ropa planchada y deslumbrante.

The Serene Haze of the Hours

Cracked bodies admonish me
to picture the sun of motionless time
in the serene shadow of the hours
that flow through the curved messages
of the ruddy accordion of the still
chest where you're stripped to the waist.
Below your skin, distance wells up
with destroyed dreams that dispel
the loquacious persistence of legends
of complex rites and memories.
I am consoled only by the contours
of forgotten and far-off remains
that survive in my thoughts
of your ironed and dazzling clothes.

El Mar de Nuestro Regreso

Sobre la cúpula nevada
la estrella y la luna refulgen
fondo rojo que desdibuja
el vuelo de tristes gaviotas.
Imposible reconocernos
como barco de la tormenta
que avanza temeroso y luce
en el cuerno de oro que fuimos.
La nieve no cubre pisadas
ni reniega de los perfiles
en el mar de nuestro recuerdo.
Juego a descubrir quienes somos
o si alguna vez habitamos
en el palpitar que destrenza
las ilusiones de la vida.

Remiendo la pena con hilos
de sol, tapiz de tu memoria.

The Sea of Our Return

Above the snow-covered dome
star and the moon shine brightly
a red background that blurs
the flight of sad seagulls.
We can not recognize each other
like a ship in a storm
that advances fearfully and shines
in the golden horn where once we traveled.
The snow does not cover footsteps
nor renounce the contours
in the sea of our remembering.
I play at discovering who we are
or if sometime we used to live
in the throbbing that untangles
the illusions of life,

I mend sorrow with threads
of sun, tapestry of your memory.

Larga Espera

Espera la flor blanca del ciruelo
a que zarpen los buques hacia el lago
a que cesen los días sin la noche
y las nubes que ordenan el granizo.
Espera que en la playa nazcan olas
con lealtades caducas de un sollozo,
a que los manantiales viertan savia
y los árboles sanen tempestades.
Espera que descubras que en tu invierno
casi siempre es verano de nostalgias
donde puedes mirar junto a tus ojos
la primavera de tu ancho suspiro.
No te vayas confusa que distante
espero que mi arrullo sea discurso
y bailemos la danza del naufragio.
Espera que mi llanto se haga viejo.

Long Wait

Wait for the white flower of the plum tree
the ships launched on the lake set sail for
where the days may end without night
and the clouds that command the hail.
Wait for waves to be born on the beach
with the old-fashioned loyalties of a sigh,
where the springs run with sap
and the trees heal storms.
Wait to discover that in your winter
there is always a summer of nostalgia
where you can watch with your own eyes
the spring of your extended sigh.
Don't become confused that from a distance
I hope that my cooing comes across as talk.
and let's dance the dance of the shipwreck.
Wait for my tears to grow old.

Un Secreto Insomne

Desnudez es la vida y desnudez la sola eternidad.
Juan Ramón Jiménez

Anidaron las garzas y te pienso
en el lugar anverso de la cumbre
del artificio, copias clandestinas,
exaltación superflua de quimeras.
En los senderos húmedos retratan
la decadente búsqueda que parte
de la falsa belleza que han soñado.
Y el sol calienta sin descanso y vibra
como la verdad pulcra y renovada
que saboreo nostalgia de la nieve,
en un mar humillado por secretos
tejidos con agujas recelosas
de mujeres tocadas por turbantes
que guardan La Torá sobre perennes
faldas inesperadas con arena.
Allí donde fracasan las heladas
y el calor es insomne, yo te pienso.

A Sleepless Secret

> *Nakedness is life and nakedness is the only eternity.*
> Juan Ramón Jiménez

Herons build their nests and I think of you
in the foremost place on the summit
of artifice, clandestine copies,
superfluous exaltation of chimeras.
On the damp paths, they portray
the decadent search that sets off
from the false beauty they have dreamed.
And the sun warms without stopping and shivers
like the beautiful renewed truth
that I can taste the nostalgia of snow,
in a sea humiliated by secrets
woven with suspicious needles
by women crowned by their turbans
who guard the Torah in their timeless
skirts surging up from the sand.
There where the frosts fail
and the heat is sleepless, I think of you.

III
Views of Winter
Las Miradas del Invierno

Los Límites Helados de Tu Ausencia

Cuando no duermes a mi lado quiebra
nuestra esencia y licuada se derrama,
malvado sedimento de inquietudes
que envejecen mis ojos aturdidos.
La noche se subleva caprichosa
extendiendo su mano por el cráter
que tu cuerpo, la escolta de mi vida,
ha dejado en los límites helados.
Los minutos se vuelven balaustrada
de los reproches que se desvanecen
al paso de los sueños que titilan
con zumbido constante por tu ausencia.
Cuando no duermes a mi lado todo
alrededor se vuelve pesadumbre
y mis costumbres son desconocidas;
lo que construimos es como el destello
de un ritual que me arrulla persistente.

Cuando mate al mosquito con mis labios
pronunciaré palabras de esperanza.

The Frozen Boundaries of Your Absence

When you are not sleeping by my side
our melted essence spills out,
a malicious sediment of worries
that age my stupefied eyes.
The night rises capriciously
extending its hand through the crater
that your body, the guardian of my life,
has left between frozen boundaries.
The minutes become a balustrade
of reproaches that fade away
when it hears the step of dreams that flutter
with a constant buzzing when you're gone.
When you are not sleeping by my side
everything around becomes a nightmare
and my habits are unrecognizable:
what we built is like the twinkling
of a ritual that persistently lulls me to sleep.

When I kill the mosquito with my lips
I will pronounce words of hope.

Paseo por la Nostalgia

> *Había caído la tarde, y llegué, por un bello y tranquilo camino o senda lateral que discurría entre árboles, al lago, y aquí termino el paseo.*
> Robert Walser

Caminaré por los parques desnudos
deshaciendo el sabor de tu sonrisa
que salpicaba de luz los zarzales
y vencía la tristeza de la nieve.

No habrá báculo que fisure el hielo
que retiene las hojas del otoño
y las atrapa en fuentes de cenizas
caños ausentes en la madrugada
ardiente de tus ojos desvelados.

Se posará el gorrión en el resquicio
de la soledad de mis pasos ciegos
y revolotearán sus ilusiones
tapizando con lágrimas la arena.

Y entonces no sabré pintar los surcos
que retratan tu nombre de nostalgia.

I Stroll Through Nostalgia

> *It was now evening and I came to a quiet, pretty path or side road which ran under trees, toward the lake, and here the walk ended.*
> Robert Walser

I will walk through naked parks
undoing the taste of your smile
that splattered brambles with light
and conquered the sadness of snow.

There will be no stick to crack the ice
to keep the leaves of autumn
and trap them in fountains of ash
absent tubes in the early morning
burning in your unsleeping eyes.

You will locate the sparrow in the crevice
of the solitude of my blind steps
and your illusions will flutter about
upholstering the sand with tears.

And then I won't know how to cover the wrinkles
that paint your name in nostalgia.

Los Sonidos Ensordecidos del Olvido

Te vencieron las nubes del invierno
cicatrices de brisa penitente
que delatan tu culpa retenida
entre los dedos que hurgan tu memoria.
Respiraste del polvo con tus años
espadas acechantes del olvido
en los sueños lavados de perdones
espuma redimida entre la niebla.
Las campanas repican desconsuelo
saludan los instantes que sollozan
péndulo de la vida derrumbada
por el acantilado de tus ojos.
Y brillan tus recuerdos transparentes
glaciar en primavera que ilumina
naufragio de un cristal ensordecido
que no emite sonidos de regreso.

¿Y si les diera forma de botella?

The Deafening Sounds of Oblivion

Clouds of winter overcome you
scars of penitent breeze
that betray the guilt you held back
between fingers rummaging through your memory.
You breathed in dust with your years
swords lying in wait for oblivion
in dreams washed with pardons
foam redeemed in the mist.
The bells chime their grief
they greet the minutes that sigh
pendulum of a life devastated
by the promontory of your eyes.
And your transparent memories shine
glacier in spring that illuminates
shipwreck of a deafened crystal
Emitting no sounds of return.

And if they had the shape of a bottle?

Las Pisadas del Frío

> *Luna, como si un alguien*
> *muerto avanzara*
> *desde la gruta azul*
> *y caen flores muchas*
> *sobre el sendero de rocas.*
> Georg Trakl

Desaparecerá la nieve grácil
y brillarán los bronces resignados
a cubrirse de blanco en los inviernos.
¡Siluetas lapidarias de la noche,
homenajes secretos que perviven!

Asomará el asfalto entre los surcos
de pisadas efímeras del aire
por un frío que regresa con prestancia
dispuesto a congelar las ataduras
del lago de deslices fugitivos.

Levantará la bruma que penetra
en los cuerpos maduros sin memoria
relicarios con briznas de ilusiones
que miran los tejados expectantes
en un vergel de sueños amputados.

Se mostrarán las ramas de los chopos
y acudirán las aves animosas
a cantar en los parques florecidos
de parejas y niños que entre risas
corretean con sus tímidos cortejos.

Y entonces, quizás seas una estrella
convertida en novia de azabache.

The Footsteps of the Cold

> *Moon, as if someone*
> *dead advanced*
> *From the blue grotto*
> *And many flowers fall*
> *Onto the rocky path.*
> Georg Trakl

The graceful snow will disappear
and the resigned bronzes will shine
covering themselves in the white of winters.
Lapidary silhouettes of night,
secret homages that endure!

Asphalt will appear in the furrows
of ephemeral airy footsteps
with a cold that elegantly returns
ready to freeze the ligatures
of the lake of fleeing indiscretions.

The penetrating mist will raise
reliquaries with wisps of illusions
in mature bodies without memory
that watch the expectant roofs
in an orchard of amputated dreams.

Black poplar branches will show
and spirited birds will come
to sing in the parks flowering
where laughing couples and children
run around in their timid courtships.

And then, perhaps you will be a star
converted into a jet-black bride.

Luz en el Invernadero

Entraste por aquel jardín de invierno
ángel etéreo de formas volubles
portador de una lira engalanada
con plegarias efímeras, hechizo
para lacayos de la diosa Flora.
En su interior vaciaste la alegría
y en el cristal crecieron calendarios
al auspicio del frío de la nieve.
Senderos con ritual inquebrantable
en mañanas lluviosas de perdones
desvelan las virtudes de palabras
oníricas de rojo sortilegio
exaltadas con flores en la niebla
relucientes al roce de caprichos
que durmieron con el candor de tu halo.
Te fundiste sutil con el deshielo
y hoy reposan escombros de pasiones
hongos de saciedad en la urna rota.
Olvidaste que el calor vendría
y con el sol, un cuervo solitario.

Light in the Greenhouse

You came in through that winter garden
ethereal angel of unstable forms
carrier of a lyre garlanded
with ephemeral prayers, a spell
for the minions of the goddess Flora.
In its interior, you emptied out joy
And in the crystal calendars grew
under the auspices of the cold of snow.
Paths with unbreakable ritual
on rainy mornings of forgiveness
keep awake the virtues of dreamlike
words of red incantation
exalted by flowers in the mist
gleaming with a touch of caprice
sleeping on the candor of your halo.
Subtly you fused yourself with the thaw
and today rubbles of passion rest
mushrooms of fullness in the broken urn.
You forgot that the heat will come
And with the sun, a solitary crow.

La Nieve de Tu Memoria

Miro por la ventana
y el agua se condensa
en el cristal, espectro
de tus pómulos frios.
Mi pensamento bulle
la gota desvalida
que se resbala obtusa
sin un destino firme.
Y recuerdo la nieve
que cubrió tu memoria
en paradero oculto,
promontorio de olvidos.
Vendrá la primavera
rebosante de nardos
y tú, ensimismada,
cimbrarás los deseos
fugaces hematomas
en combate de hormigas.

The Snow of Your Memory

I look through the window
and water condenses
in the crystal, a ghost
of your cold cheekbones.
My thought boils
the defenseless droplet
that darkly slides
with no place to go.
And I remember the snow
That covered your memory
in a hidden location,
promontory of oblivion.
The Spring will come
brimming with spikenards
and you, self-absorbed,
will bend desires,
ephemeral bruises
in combat with ants.

Sueños Premonitorios

Arrasado por un tornado queda
la esperada condena del silencio
alijo de impaciencias de un letargo
que te ensordece de vacuos pesares.

Volverás a ver un mar que te entregue
la quietud reservada con la noche
espejo rescatado de fragmentos
celadores de sueños ateridos.

Y me pides que te cante pasiones
para cauterizar la herida antigua
perdida en la espesura de un invierno
que sepultó las huellas del pasado.

Vives y sin embargo mi memoria
se adelanta a tu muerte aventurada.

Premonitory Dreams

Flattened by a tornado the expected
sentence of silence remains
offloading of impatience of a lethargy
deafening you with empty regrets.

You will see again a sea delivering
discreet calm to you with nighttime
a mirror reconstructed from fragments
keeping watch over frozen dreams.

And you ask me to sing you passions
to cauterize the ancient wound
lost in the density of a winter
that buried the traces of the past.

Even as you live my memory
rushes toward the risk of your death.

WINTERREISE

Se cerró el firmamento de tus ojos
párpados compasivos del instante
que vela la memoria congelada.
Terminaste tu viaje del invierno
dormida bajo un cielo sin epílogo
cristal opaco de tus manos muertas.
Lo supe al escuchar la voz errante
en el mar que te quiso misteriosa
y en el camino lleno de jilgueros
posados en las ramas impacientes
de árboles que supuran horizontes.
La luna sangra con la noche estéril
el tiempo liberado de olas negras
y náufragos silentes que dormitan.
Al ver la placidez clara en tu rostro
lágrimas de colores punzan mi alma.

Winterreise

The firmament of your eyes closed
compassionate eyelids of the instant
that kept awake the frozen memory.
You ended your winter journey
while I slept under a sky without epilogue
opaque crystal in your dead hands.
I knew it on hearing the wandering voice
In the sea that loved the mystery of you
and in the road filled with finches
perching on impatient branches
of trees extending over the horizon.
The moon bleeds with sterile night
time freed from black waves
silent shipwrecks that sleep.
When I see the clear placidity in your face
tears of colors pierce my soul.

About the Author

Alicia Aza, by profession an attorney specializing in corporate law in Madrid, has published four books of poems. Both *El libro de los árboles* and *Las Huellas fértiles* (2014) were nominated as finalists for the Andalusian Premio de la Crítica. *El viaje del invierno* (2011) won the International Rosalía de Castro Poetry Prize. *Arquitectura del silencio* (*Architecture of Silence*) was published by Valparaíso Editions first in the original Spanish only (2017) and then in a bilingual edition in 2018. Aza's literary work has appeared in many international journals and anthologies and been translated into Arabic, Bulgarian, French, Italian, and Serbian, as well as into English. She is a member of the Writers' Association of Spain and vice president of La Asociación Internacional Humanismo Solidario.

About the Translators

J. Kates is a minor poet, an award-winning literary translator of Russian and French poetry and the co-director of Zephyr Press. He has been granted three National Endowment for the Arts Fellowships and an Individual Artist Fellowship from the New Hampshire State Council on the Arts. He has published three chapbooks of his own poems and one full book, *The Briar Patch* (Hobblebush Books). He is also the translator of a dozen books of Russian and French poetry, has edited two anthologies of translations, and collaborated with Stephen A. Sadow on a half dozen books of Latin American and Peninsular Spanish poetry in translation.

Stephen A. Sadow is Professor Emeritus of Latin American Literature and Jewish Studies at Northeastern University in Boston. He specializes in Latin American Jewish literature and art. Among Sadow's books are *King David's Harp: Autobiographical Essays by Jewish Latin American Writers*, winner of a National Jewish Book Award and his translations of *Mestizo, A Novel* by Ricardo Feierstein, *Unbroken: From Auschwitz to Buenos Aires*, the autobiography of Holocaust survivor Charles Papiernik, and *Philosophy and other Fables*, short essays by Isaac Goldemberg. With J. Kates, he has co-translated poetry by César Tiempo, Teodoro Ducach, Rosita Kalina, Angelina Muñiz-Huberman, Miryam Gover de Nasatsky, Ricardo Feierstein, José Pivín, Isaac Goldemberg, Susana Grimberg, Daniel Chirom, Sonia Chocrón, and Alicia Aza.

CPSIA information can be obtained
at www.ICGtesting.com
Printed in the USA
FSHW020128040620
70659FS

9 781950 063369